Sensual Wit With Bedi

Sensual Wit With Bedi

Ran Bedi

Bigfoot Publications
Because, there's a writer in everyone.

Sensual Wit With Bedi

Author : Ran Bedi

First Published by
Bigfoot06 Publications (OPC) Pvt. Ltd. B-10,12 Shree Shyam Palace, Sector 4,5 Chowk, Old Railway Road, Gurugram, Haryana (122001)
Website: www.bigfootpublications.in Email: info@bigfootpublications.in

First Edition : September, 2023

ISBN Print Book - **978-81-19201-90-7**

Printed in India

Dedicated to all my naughty friends who believed in themselves and lived their lives to the fullest.

Preface

On retirement, the author, an army officer and subsequently served in security industry. Travelled worldwide, his life has been full of struggle, risks and dangers. Having survived close skirmishes with death, he started observing humour in day-to-day life.

The book is about bringing light-hearted fun & humour as observed in daily life. There are jokes about Golf, Tennis and Bridge - games that the author pursued in his army career. The book has been collated by observing routine life experiences; with the prism of laughter and smiles.

The inspiration was derived from the famous magazine "Reader's Digest" viz., 'Laughter - The Best Medicine', 'Life's Like That' and Humour in Uniform.

Humour & Insults

These glorious insults are from an era before the English language boiled down to 4-letter words.

The exchange between Churchill & Lady Astor:

She said, "If you were my husband, I'd give you poison." He said,

"If you were my wife, I'd drink it."

😍

A Member of Parliament to Disraeli: "Sir, you will either die on the gallows or of some unspeakable disease."

"That depends, Sir," said Disraeli, "whether I embrace your policies or your mistress."

😍

Wicked Humour

John asks his grandpa: "Do you still have sex with Granny?"

Grandpa says: "Yes, but only Oral."

John says: "What is oral?"

Grandpa: "I say F**k you," and she says, "F**k you too."

😍

The 3 tragedies in a man's life:

1- Life sucks
2- Job sucks
3- Wife does NOT!

😍

A man is dying of cancer.

His son: Dad why do you keep telling people you're dying of AIDS?

Answer: So that when I die, no one will dare to f**k your mother.

😍

Yesterday's News: A nun jogging in the park was raped. Today's News: Hundreds of nuns are jogging in the park!

😍

Question: "Why is a waist called a waist?""

Answer: "Because anything above the p**sy and below the tits is a waste."

😍

Question: "What's common between a good-looking, faithful, rich husband who satisfies his wife sexually every night and Bin Laden?"

Answer: "BOTH CANNOT BE FOUND"

😍

Everything on a female's upper body starts with - B

"B" - Blouse, Bra, Bikini, B (.)(.)Bs.

Lower body with - P

"P" - Petticoat, Pants, Panties, P*ssy. No wonder men get "BP" problems.

😍

Salary Rise By Penis

I, the penis, hereby request a raise in salary for the following reasons:

* I do physical labour.
* I work at great depths.
* I work headfirst.
* I do not get weekends off or public holidays.
* I work in a damp environment.
* I don`t get paid overtime or shift penalties.
* I work in a dark workplace that has poor ventilation.
* I work in high temperatures.
* My work exposes me to contagious diseases.

Response from the Administration

After assessing your request and considering the arguments you have raised. The administration rejects your request for the following reasons:

* You do not work 8 hours straight.
* You fall asleep on the job after brief work periods.
* You do not always follow the orders of the management team.
* You do not stay in your allocated position and often visit other areas.
* You take a lot of non-rostered breaks.

* You do not take initiative - you need to be pressured and stimulated in order to start working.

* You leave the workplace rather messy at the end of your shift.

* You don`t always observe WH&S (Work Health & Safety) measures, such as wearing the correct protective outfits.

* You don`t wait till pension age before retiring.

* You don`t like working double shifts.

* You sometimes leave your allocated position before you have completed the day`s work.

* And if that were not all, you have been seen constantly entering and leaving the work place carrying 2 suspicious- looking bags.

😍

The Answers We Have All Been Waiting For!

Q: What are the small bumps around a woman's nipples for? A: It's Braille for 'suck here'.

Q: What is an Australian kiss?
A: It's the same as a French kiss, but 'down under.'

Q: What do you do with 365 used condoms?
A: Melt them down, make a tire, and call it a Good Year.

Q: Why were hurricanes normally named after women?
A: Because when they come, they're wild and wet. But when they go, they take your house and car with them.

Q: Why do girls rub their eyes when they get up in the morning? A: Because they don't have any balls to scratch...

Q: What is a man's Ultimate embarrassment?
A: Running into a wall with an erection and breaking his nose.

😍

Nominated as the world's best short JOKE !!

A 3-year-old boy examined his testicles while taking a bath. Mom, he asked, “Are these my brains?”

“Not yet,” she replied.

😍

The Top 10 Things That Sound Dirty, But In A Law Firm, Are Not:

1. Have you looked through her briefs?
2. He is one hard judge.
3. Counsellor - “Let's do it in chambers.”
4. Her attorney withdrew at the last minute.
5. Is it a penal offence?
6. Better leave the handcuffs on.
7. For $200 an hour, she better be good!
8. Can you get him to drop his suit?
9. The judge gave her the stiffest one he could.
10. Think you can get me off?

😍

Top 10 Things That Sound Dirty, But In The Office, Are Not:

10. I need to whip it out by 5.

9. Mind if I use your laptop?

8. Just stick it in my box.

7. If I have to lick one more, I'll gag!

6. I want it on my desk, NOW!!!!!

5. HMMMMM, I think it's out of fluid!

4. My equipment is so old; it takes forever to finish.

3. It's an entry-level position.

2. When do you think you'll be getting off today?

And the number 1 thing that sounds dirty but at the office isn't

1. It's not fair. I do all the work while he just sits there!!!

😍

Brain Teasers

Q. What's the difference between cricketers and condoms?

A: Cricketers drop the catches and condoms catches the drops.

Q: What is the difference between riding a bicycle and a woman?

A: Riding a bicycle you fix your ass & move your legs, riding a woman you fix your legs & move your ass.

Q: What three things are common between the sun and woman's underwear?

A: Both are hot, both look better while going down and both disappear at night.

Q: Why do men ask for a woman's hand in marriage? A: Because they are tired of using their own.

Q: What's common between men and video?

A: Both go backward... forward... backward... forward... backward.... forward... stop and eject.

Q: What is the closest thing similar to a woman's period?

A: Your salary, it comes once a month, lasts about 5-7 days and if it doesn't come means you are in big trouble.

Q: What goes in dry, comes out wet, and gives warm satisfaction?

A: A teabag.

😍

7 Qualities To Be a Perfect Wife:

Beautiful

Responsible

Energetic

Adorable

Sweet

Truthful

Self-Organized

In short, she must have good B.R.E.A.S.T.S

😍

Q: Who is a gynecologist?

A: He is the only fool on the earth who looks for problems in a place, where most people find pleasure.

Q: What is the similarity between men and rats?

A: Both keep searching for new HOLES.

Q: What's the difference between biology and sociology?

A: When the baby looks like his dad, then it is biology. When the baby looks like a neighbour, then it is sociology.

Q: What's the height of recycling?

A: Sending a sanitary napkin for dry cleaning.

Doctor: You look so weak & exhausted. Are you having 3 meals a day as I have advised?

Lady: Doctor, I thought you had said 3 males a day.

Girlfriend & boyfriend go for a movie. In the dark, a mosquito enters the girl's skirt. Guess where it would have bitten?

The boy's hand......

The secret of long life...

Morning two eggs, evening two pegs......and night between two legs

😍

Humour & Golf

Wife of a Golfer Saturday morning!

I got up early, dressed quietly, made my lunch, grabbed my golf bag, tried not to wake my wife, sneaked quietly into the garage and proceeded to back out into a torrential down pour.

The wind was blowing 50 mph. I pulled back into the garage, turned on the radio, and discovered that the weather would be bad throughout the day.

Disappointed I went back into the house, quietly undressed, and sneaked back into bed. There I cuddled up to my wife's back, now with a different anticipation, and whispered, 'The weather out there is terrible."

My loving wife of 20 years replied, "Can you believe my stupid husband is out there playing golf in that terrible weather?"

I still don't know to this day if she was joking, but I have stopped playing golf.

😍

Top 10 Things That Sound Dirty, But In Golf, Are Not:

10. Damn, my shaft is bent.

9. After 18 holes, I can barely walk.

8. You really whacked the hell out of that sucker.

7. Look at the size of his putter.

6. Keep your head down and spread your legs a bit more.

5. Mind if I join your threesome?

4. Stand with your back turned and drop it.

3. My hands are so sweaty I can't get a good grip!

2. Nice stroke, but your follow-through leaves a lot to be desired.

And the number 1 thing that sounds dirty but in golf isn't

1. Hold up! I need to wash my balls first!

😍

Golf Nut

John and Helen met while on vacation, and John fell head over heels in love with her. And after a couple of weeks in which John took Helen out that it was true love.

So.....on the last night of his vacation, the two of them went to dinner and had a serious talk about how the relationship would continue. "It's only fair to warn you, I'm a total golf nut," John said to his new-found lady friend... "I eat, sleep and breathe golf, so if that's going to be a problem, you'd better say so now!"

Helen took a deep breath and responded: "Since we're being honest with each other, you need to know that I'm a **hooker.**"

"I see," John replied. "That's a problem, for sure." He spent some time looking down at the table, deep in thought. Then he said, "You know, it's probably because you're not keeping your wrists straight when you tee off."

😍

Golf Balls

I was at the golf store comparing different kinds of golf balls. I was unhappy with the women's type I had been using.

After browsing for several minutes, I was approached by one of the good-looking gentlemen who works at the store.

He asked if he could help me. Without thinking, I looked at him and said, "I think I like playing with men’s balls."

😍

Bee Stings

A young woman had been taking golf lessons.

She had just started playing her first round of golf when she suffered a bee sting.

Her pain was so intense that she decided to return to the clubhouse for help and to complain.

Her golf pro saw her come into the clubhouse and asked, “Why are you back in so early? What's wrong?”

“I was stung by a bee,” she said. “Where?” he asked. “Between the first and second hole,” she replied.

He nodded knowingly and said, “Then your stance is too wide.”

😍

Tee off

After 25 years of marriage, Jacqueline and her husband Marc went for counseling. When asked what the problem was, Jacqueline went into a passionate, painful tirade listing every problem they had ever had in the 25 years they had been married. She went on and on and on about neglect, lack of intimacy, emptiness, loneliness, feeling unloved and unlovable, an entire laundry list of unmet needs she had endured over the course of their marriage.

Finally, after allowing this to go on for a sufficient length of time, the therapist got up, walked around the desk and, after asking Jacqueline to stand, he unbuttoned her blouse, embraced her, put his hands on her breasts, and kissed her passionately as her husband Marc watched with a raised eyebrow. Jacqueline shut up, buttoned up her blouse, and quietly sat down as though in a daze.

The therapist turned to Marc and said, "This is what your wife needs at least three times a week."

Can you do this?

Marc thought for a moment and replied, "Well, I can drop her off here on Mondays and Wednesdays, but on Fridays, I play golf."

😍

Golf addict

"I was asked by a golfer how to lower his scores. I replied start playing 9 holes instead of 18. It worked for me to cut my scores in half." - Brian Weis.

"There are three roads to ruin: women, gambling, and golf. The most pleasant is with women, the quickest is with gambling, but the surest is with golf."

- Andrew Perry

😍

Groin Massage

Two women were playing golf. One teed off and watched in horror as her ball headed directly toward a foursome of men playing the next hole. The ball hit one of the men. He immediately clasped his hands together at his groin, fell to the ground and proceeded to roll around in agony.

The woman rushed down to the man and immediately began to apologize.

"Please allow me to help. I'm a physical therapist and I know I could relieve your pain if you'd allow me," she told him.

"Oh, no, I'll be all right. I'll be fine in a few minutes," the man replied.

He was in obvious agony, lying in a fetal position, still clasping his hands together at his groin. At her persistence, however, he finally allowed her to help.

She gently took his hands away and laid them at his side, loosened his pants and put her hands inside. She administered tender and artful massage for several long moments and asked, "How does that feel?"

He replied, "It feels great, but I still think my thumb's broken."

Christmas Gift

After her game of golf, a lady player offered her caddy a ride into town. The caddy thankfully accepted, and when they arrived at her house, he carried her clubs inside.

The lady invited him to stay for lunch and served him a wonderful meal.

She then invited him into the bedroom. He was puzzled but went along out of curiosity. She asked if he wanted to go to bed with her, so he did that too. Later he realized it was time to get back to the course and prepared to leave. The housewife insisted on giving him a dollar before he could go.

Well, it was too much for the poor man, and he asked her, "Lady, what is going on? First, you feed me a delicious meal, and as if that isn't enough, you invite me to make love to you and we have a terrific time together. Now you want to pay me?! What is this, anyway?"

She explained proudly, "Well, you know Christmas is coming, and I told my husband I wanted to do something nice for my caddy who is so faithful and helped me so much this year. My husband said, 'Screw the caddy! Give him a dollar! The lunch was my idea!"

😍

Golf Panties

The Swede's wife steps up to the tee and, as she bends over to place her ball, a gust of wind blows her skirt up and reveals her lack of underwear.

"Good God, woman! Why aren't you wearing any skivvies?" Ole demanded. "Well, you don't give me enough housekeeping money to afford any."

The Swede immediately reaches into his pocket and says, "For the sake of decency, here's a 50. Go and buy yourself some underwear."

Next, the Irishman's wife bends over to set her ball on the tee. Her skirt also blows up to show that she, too, is wearing no undies.

"Blessed Virgin Mary, woman! You've no knickers. Why not?'"

She replies, "I can't afford any on the money you give me."

Patrick reaches into his pocket and says, "For the sake of decency, here's a 20. Go and buy yourself some underwear!"

Lastly, the Scotsman's wife bends over. The wind also takes her skirt over her head to reveal that she, too, is naked under it.

"Sweet Mudder of Jaysus, Aggie! Where ta friggin hell are yer drawers?"

She too explains, "You dinna give me enough money ta be able ta affarrd any." The Scotsman reaches into his pocket and says, "Well, fer the love 'o decency, here's a comb Tidy yerself up a bit."

😍

Honeymoon Confession

A couple was on their honeymoon, lying in bed, about ready to consummate their marriage, when the new bride says to the husband, "I have a confession to make, I'm not a virgin."

The husband replies, "That's no big thing in this day and age." The

wife continues, "Yeah, I've been with one other guy." "Oh yeah?

Who was the guy?"

- "Tiger Woods."

"Tiger Woods, the golfer?"

- "Yeah."

"Well, he's rich, famous and handsome. I can see why you went to bed with him."

The husband and wife then make passionate love. When they get done, the husband gets up and walks to the telephone.

"What are you doing?" says the wife.

The husband says, "I'm hungry, I was going to call room service and get some food."

"Tiger wouldn't do that."

"Oh yeah? What would Tiger do?"

"He'd come back to bed and do it a second time."

The husband puts down the phone and goes back to bed to make love with his wife a second time. When they finish, he gets up and goes over to the phone.

"What are you doing?" she says.

The husband says, "I'm still hungry so I was going to get room service to get some food."

"Tiger wouldn't do that."

"Oh yeah? What would Tiger do?"

"He'd come back to bed and do it one more time."

The guy slams down the phone and goes back to bed and makes love to his wife one more time. When they finish he's tired and beat.

He drags himself over to the phone and starts to dial. The wife asks,

"Are you calling room service?"

"No! I'm calling Tiger Woods to find out what's par for this hole."

Resting The Balls

On a golf tour in Newfoundland, Canada, Tiger Woods drives his new **Ford** Fusion into a petrol station in a remote part of the countryside.

The pump attendant, who obviously knows nothing about golf, greets him completely unaware of who the golfing pro is.

"Top of the morning to you, sir," says the attendant. Tiger nods a quick hello and bends forward to pick up the nozzle. As he does so, two tees fall out of his shirt pocket onto the ground.

"What are those?" asks the attendant. "They're called tees," replies

Tiger.

"Well, what on God's earth are they for?" inquires the attendant.

"They're for resting my balls on when I'm driving," says Tiger.

"Fookin Jeysus," says the Newfoundlander, "**Ford** thinks of everything!"

😍

Santa & Tiger Woods

Warning:

Avoid being Scammed ...NASTY SCAM!!!!!! Just got scammed outta $25. I Bought Tiger Woods' DVD entitled "My Favourite 18 Holes". Turns out it's about golf. Damn, waste of money.

Pass this on so others don't get scammed!!

😍

What is the difference between Santa Claus & Tiger Woods. Santa stops after 3 Ho's (Whores).

😍

Notice At Army Golf Club

"Players will bring their own balls; however, General's (GOC) Balls will be carried by Commanding Officer Engineer Regiment... (who was in-charge of the Golf Course!)

😍

Public Notice at a Golf Course

Any person (except players) caught collecting golf balls on this course will be prosecuted and have their balls removed.

😍

Woman Golfer & the Frog

A Woman was out golfing one day when she hit the ball into the woods. She went into the woods to look for it and found a frog in a trap. The frog said to her, "If you release me from this trap, I will grant you three wishes."

The woman freed the frog, and the frog said, "Thank you, but I failed to mention the condition to your wishes. Whatever you wish for, your husband will get times ten!" The woman said, "That's okay."

For her first wish, she wanted to be the most beautiful woman in the world. The frog warned her, "You do realize that this wish will also make your husband the most handsome man in the world, an Adonis whom women will flock to." The woman replied, "That's okay because I will be the most beautiful Woman and he will have eyes only for me."

So, KAZAM-she's the most beautiful Woman in the world! For her second wish, she wanted to be the richest woman in the world. The frog said, "That will make your husband the richest man in the world. And he will be ten times richer than you. "The woman said, "That's okay, because what's mine is his and what's his is mine." So, KAZAM-she's the richest woman in the world!

The frog then inquired about her third wish, and she answered, "I'd like a mild heart attack."

Moral of the story: Women are clever. Don't mess with them.
Attention female readers: This is the end of the joke for you. Stop here and continue feeling good. Male readers: *Next Page *

The man had a heart attack ten times milder than his wife!!! Moral of the story:

Women think they're really smart, let them continue to think that way and just enjoy the show.

PS: If you are a woman and are still reading this; it only goes to show that women never listen!!!

😍

Golfer at the Dentist!

A man and his wife walked into a dentist's office. The man said to the dentist, “Doc, I'm in one heck of a hurry. I have two buddies sitting out in my car waiting for us to go play golf, so forget about the anesthetic, just pull the tooth, and be done with it. We have a 10:00 am tee time at the best golf course in town and it's 9:30 already. I don't have time to wait for the anesthetic to work!” The dentist thought to himself, My goodness, this is surely a very brave man asking to have his tooth pulled without using anything to kill the pain. So the dentist asks him, “Which tooth is it, sir?” The man turned to his wife and said, “Open your mouth Honey, and show him.”

😍

Old Golfer

A crusty old golfer comes in from a round of golf at a new course and heads into the grill room. As he passes through the swinging door, he sees a sign hanging over the bar:

COLD BEER:	$2.00
HAMBURGER:	$2.25
CHEESEBURGER:	$2.50
CHICKEN SANDWICH:	$3.50
HAND JOB:	$50.00

Checking his wallet to be sure he has the necessary payment, the old golfer walks up to the bar and beckons to the exceptionally attractive female bartender who is serving drinks to a couple of sun-wrinkled golfers. She glides down behind the bar to the old golfer.

"Yes?" she inquires with a wide, knowing smile, "May I help you?" The old golfer leans over the bar, "I was wondering, young lady," he whispers, "Are you the one who gives the hand- jobs?"

She looks into his eyes with that wide smile and purrs: "Yes Sir, I sure am."

The old golfer leans closer and into her left ear whispers softly, "Well, wash your hands real fucking good, 'cause I want a cheeseburger and a beer."

😍

10 Best Golf Caddy Remarks.

#10
Golfer: "Think I'm going to drown myself in the lake." Caddy: "Think you can keep your head down that long?"

#9
Golfer: "I'd move heaven and earth to break 100 on this course."
Caddy: "Try heaven, you've already moved most of the earth."

#8
Golfer: "Do you think my game is improving?" Caddy: "Yes sir, you miss the ball much closer now."

#7
Golfer: "Do you think I can get there with a 5 iron?" Caddy: "Eventually."

#6
Golfer: "You've got to be the worst caddy in the world." Caddy: "I don't think so sir. That would be too much of a Coincidence."

#5
Golfer: "Please stop checking your watch all the time. It's too much of a distraction."
Caddy: "It's not a watch - it's a compass."

#4
Golfer: "How do you like my game?"
Caddy: "Very good sir, but personally, I prefer golf."

#3
Golfer: "Do you think it's a sin to play on Sunday?" Caddy: "The way you play, sir, it's a sin on any day."

#2
Golfer: "This is the worst course I've ever played on." Caddy: "This isn't the golf course. We left that an hour ago."

#1 Best Caddy Comment:
Golfer: "That can't be my ball, it's too old."
Caddy: "It's been a long time since we teed off, sir."

😍

The Caddy

And the old favorite.....is the one about the Golfer who has been slicing off the tee at every hole.

He finally gives up and asks his long-suffering caddy if he has seen any obvious problems to which the caddy replies.

“There's a bit of shit on the end of your club Sir.”

The Golfer picks his club up and cleans the club face at which point the caddy says,“The other end, Sir.”

😍

Stranded Irishman

One day an Irishman who had been stranded on a deserted island for over 10 years, saw a speck on the horizon. He thought to himself, "It's certainly not a ship." And, as the speck got closer and closer, he began to rule out the possibilities of a small boat or even a raft.

Suddenly there emerged from the surf a wet-suited black-clad figure. Putting aside the scuba gear and the top of the wet suit, there stood a drop-dead gorgeous blonde! The glamorous blonde strode up to the stunned Irishman and said to him, "Tell me, how long has it been since you've had a cigarette?"

"Ten years," replied the amazed Irishman. With that, she reached over and unzipped a waterproofed pocket on the left sleeve of her wet suit and pulled out a fresh pack of cigarettes. He takes one, lights it, and takes a long drag. "Faith and begorra," said the man, "that is so good I'd almost forgotten how great a smoke can be!"

"And how long has it been since you've had a drop of good Irish whiskey," asked the blonde.

Trembling, the castaway replied, "Ten years." Hearing that, the blonde reaches over to her right sleeve unzips a pocket there and removes a flask and hands it to him. He opened the flask and took a long drink.

"Tis nectar of the gods!" stated the Irishman. "Tis truly fantastic!!!"

At this point, the gorgeous blonde started to slowly unzip the long front of her wet suit, right down the middle. She looked at the trembling man and asked, "And how long has it been since you played around?"

With tears in his eyes, the Irishman fell to his knees and sobbed; "Sweet Jaysus! Don't tell me you've got golf clubs in there too!"

😍

Second Testimony

I was at the golf store comparing different kinds of golf balls. I was unhappy with the women's type I had been using.
After browsing for several minutes,
I was approached by one of the good-looking gentlemen who works at the store.
He asked if he could help me.
Without thinking, I looked at him and said, "I think I like playing with men's balls."

😍

Father, Son & Grandson

A father, son and grandson went to the country club for their weekly round of golf. Just as they reached the first tee, a beautiful young blonde woman carrying her bag of clubs approached them.

She explained that the member who brought her to the club for a round of golf had an emergency that called him away and asked the trio whether she could join them.

Naturally, all the guys agreed.

Smiling, the blonde thanked them and said, “Look, fellows, I work in a topless bar as a dancer, so nothing shocks me anymore. If any of you want to smoke cigars, have a beer, bet, swear, tell off-color stories, or do anything that you normally do when playing a round together, go ahead. But, I enjoy playing golf, consider myself pretty good at it, so don't try to coach me on how to play my shots.”

With that, the guys agreed to relax and invited her to drive first.

All eyes were fastened on her shapely behind as she bent to place her ball on the tee. She then took her driver and hit the ball 270 yards down the middle, right in front of the green.

The father's mouth was agape. “That was beautiful,” he said.

The blonde put her driver away and said, “I really didn't get into it, and I faded it a little.”

After the three guys hit their drives and their second shots, the blonde took out an eight iron and lofted the ball within five feet of the hole (She was closest to the pin.)

The son said, “Damn, lady, you played that perfectly.”

The blonde frowned and said, “It was a little weak, but even an easy seven would have been too much club. I've left a tricky little putt.” She then tapped in the five-footer for a birdie.

Having the honours, she drove first on the second hole, knocked the heck out of the ball, and it landed nearly 300 yards away smack in the middle of the fairway.

For the rest of the round, the statuesque blonde continued to amaze the guys, quietly and methodically shooting for par or less on every hole.

When they arrived at the 18th green, the blonde was three under par and had a very nasty 12-foot putt on an undulating green for a par.

She turned to the three guys and said, "I really want to thank you all for not acting like a bunch of chauvinists and telling me what club to use or how to play a shot, but I need this putt for a 69 and I'd really like to break 70 on this course.

If any one of you can tell me how to make par on this hole I'll take him back to my apartment, pour some 35-year-old Single Malt Strathmill Scotch in him, fix him a steak dinner, and then show him a very good time the rest of the night."

The yuppie son jumped at the thought! He strolled across the green, carefully eyeing the line of the putt and finally said, "Honey, aim about 6 inches to the right of the hole and hit it firm. It will get over that little hump and break right into the cup."

The father knelt and sighted the putt using his putter as a plumb. "Don't listen to the kid, darlin', you want to hit it softly 10 inches to the right and let it run left down that little hogback, so it falls into the cup."

The old gray-haired grandfather walked over to the blonde's ball, picked it up and handed it to her and said, "That's a gimme, sweetheart."

The blonde smiled and said, "Your car or mine?"

Old Age & Treachery Will Overcome Youth & Skill Every Time..!

😍

David Letterman's Top 10 Reasons – Why Golf Is Better Than Sex.

#10... A below-par performance is considered damn good.

#9. You can stop in the middle and have a cheeseburger and a couple of beers.

#8. It's much easier to find the sweet spot. #7. Foursomes are

encouraged.

#6. You can still make money doing it as a senior.

#5. Three times a day is possible.

#4. Your partner doesn't hire a lawyer if you play with someone else.

#3. If you live in Florida, you can do it almost every day.

#2. You don't have to cuddle with your partner when you're finished.

And the Number one reason why golf is better than sex......

#1. If your equipment gets old and rusty, you can replace it!

😍

Accounts

The owner of a golf course was confused about paying an invoice, so he decided to ask his secretary for some mathematical help. He called her into his office and said, “You graduated from the University of Tennessee, and I need some help. If I were to give you $20,000, minus 14%, how much would you take off?” She replied: "Everything but my earrings!"

Fore!

My five-year-old nephew wanted to caddy for my brother's golf game.
"You have to count my strokes," my brother told him. "How much is six plus nine plus eight?"
"Five," answered the nephew. "Okay," my brother said, "let's go."

Scratch Golfer

Two women were put together as partners in the club tournament and met on the putting green for the first time.

After introductions, the first golfer asked, "What's your handicap?"

"Oh, I'm a scratch golfer," the other replied.

"Really!" exclaimed the first woman suitably impressed that she was paired up with her. "Yes, I write down all my good scores and scratch out the bad ones!"

😍

Doctor

A husband and wife are on the 9th green when suddenly she collapses from a heart attack! "Help me dear," she groans to her husband.

The husband calls 911 on his cell phone, talks for a few minutes, picks up his putter, and lines up his putt. His wife raises her head off the green and stares at him. "I'm dying here and you're putting?"

"Don't worry dear," says the husband calmly, " they found a doctor on the second hole and he's coming to help you."

"Well, how long will it take for him to get here," she asks feebly. "No time at all," says her husband.

"Everybody's already agreed to let him play through!"

😍

Numbers

A gushy reporter told Phil Michelson, "You are spectacular, your name is synonymous with the game of golf. You really know your way around the course. What's your secret?"

Michelson replied, "The holes are numbered!"

😍

Priest

A young man and a priest are playing together. At a short par-3, the priest asks, "What are you going to use on this hole my son?"

The young man says, "An 8-iron, father. How about you?" The priest says, "I'm going to hit a soft seven and pray."

The young man hits his 8-iron and puts the ball on the green. The

priest tops his 7-iron and dribbles the ball out a few yards.
The young man says, "I don't know about you father, but in my church, when we pray, we keep our heads down!"

😍

Police

Police are called to an apartment and find a woman holding a bloody 5-iron standing over a lifeless man.

The detective asks, "Ma'am, is that your husband?" "Yes," says the woman.

"Did you hit him with that golf club?"

"Yes, yes, I did." The woman begins to sob, drops the club, and puts her, hands on her face.

"How many times did you hit him?"

"I don't know, five, six, maybe seven times, just put me down for a five!"

😍

Bride

The bride was escorted down the aisle and when she reached the altar, the groom was standing there with his golf bag and clubs at his side.

She said: "What are your golf clubs doing here?"

He looked her right in the eye and said, "This isn't going to take all day, is it?"

😍

Golfer's choice.......

Frank and his buddies were hanging out and planning a 5-day golf trip. Unfortunately, he had to tell them that he couldn't go because his wife wouldn't let him.

After a lot of teasing and name-calling, Frank headed home totally frustrated. The following week when Frank's buddies arrived at the golf resort, they were shocked to see Frank sitting in the lobby, drinking a beer, holding his putter!

"How did you talk your wife into letting you go, Frank?"

"I didn't have to," Frank replied. "Last night I slumped down in my chair with a beer to drown my sorrows. Then, my wife snuck up behind me and covered my eyes and said, 'Surprise!'
When I peeled her hands back, she was standing there in a beautiful see-through negligee and said, "Carry me into the bedroom and tie me to the bed, and you can do whatever you want .... SO HERE I AM !!"

😍

Golf – Series of Tragedies

Golf can best be defined as an endless series of tragedies obscured by the occasional miracle, followed by a good bottle of beer.

Golf! You hit down to make the ball go up. You swing left and the ball goes right. The lowest score wins. And on top of that, the winner buys the drinks.

If you find you do not mind playing golf in the rain, the snow, or even during a hurricane, here's a valuable tip: your life is in trouble.

Golfers who try to make everything perfect before taking the shot rarely make a perfect shot.

The term 'mulligan' is really a contraction of the phrase 'maul it again.'

A 'gimme' can best be defined as an agreement between two golfers ...neither of whom can putt very well.

An interesting thing about golf is that no matter how badly you play; it is always possible to get worse.

Golf's a hard game to figure. One day you'll go out and slice it and shank it, hit into all the traps and miss every green. The next day you go out and for no reason at all you really stink.

If your best shots are the practice swing and the 'gimme putt', you might wish to reconsider this game.

Golf is the only sport where the most feared opponent is you.

Golf is like marriage. If you take yourself too seriously it won't work, and both are expensive.

The best wood in most amateurs' bags is the pencil.

Lawyer Golfers

4 lawyers in a law firm lived and died for their Saturday morning round of golf. It was their favorite moment of the week. Then one of the lawyers was transferred to an office in another city. It wasn't quite the same without him.

A new woman lawyer joined their law firm. One day, she overheard the remaining three talking about their golf round at the coffee table. Curious, she spoke up, "You know, I played on my college golf team, and I was pretty good. Would you mind if I joined you next week?"

The lawyers looked at each other hesitantly. Not one of them wanted to say 'yes', but finally one of them said it would be okay, but they would be starting early at 6:30 am. He figured the early Tee-Time would discourage her immediately.

The woman said this might be a problem and asked if she could possibly be up to 15 minutes late. They rolled their eyes but said this would be okay. She smiled and said, 'Good, then I'll be there either at 6:30 or 6:45.'

She showed up right at 6:30 and wound up beating all three of them with an eye-opening 2-under-par round. She was a fun and pleasant person the entire round. The guys were impressed!

Back in the clubhouse they congratulated her and happily invited her back the next week. She smiled and said, "Sure, I'll be here at 6:30 or 6:45."

The next week, she again showed up at 6:30 Saturday morning. Only this time, she played left-handed.

The 3 lawyers were incredulous as she still managed to beat them with an even par round despite playing with her off-hand.

By now the guys were totally amazed, but wondered if she was just trying to make them look bad by beating them left-handed. They couldn't figure her out. She was again very pleasant and didn't seem to be showing them up, but each man began to harbor a burning desire to beat her!

In the 3rd week, they all had their game faces on. But this week she was 15 minutes late! This had the guys irritable because each was determined to play the best round of golf of his life to beat her. As they waited for her, they figured her late arrival was some petty gamesmanship on her part.

Finally, she showed up. This week, the lady lawyer played right-handed which was a good thing, since she narrowly beat all three of them. However, she was so gracious and so complimentary of their strong play, it was hard to keep a grudge against her. This woman was a riddle no one could figure out!

Back in the clubhouse, she had all 3 guys shaking their heads at her ability. They had a couple of beers after their round which helped the conversation loosen up.

Finally, one of the men could contain his curiosity no longer. He asked her point blank, "How do you decide if you're going to golf right-handed or left-handed?"

The lady blushed and grinned. She said, "That's easy. When my dad taught me to play golf, I learned I was ambidextrous. I have always had fun switching back and forth. Then when I met my husband in college and got married, I discovered he always sleeps in the nude. From then on, I developed a silly habit. Right before I left in the morning for golf practice, I would pull the covers off him. If his you-know-what was pointing to the right, I golfed right-handed; if it was pointed to the left, I golfed left- handed."

All the guys on the team thought this was hysterical. Astonished at this bizarre information, one of the guys shot back, "But what if it's pointed straight up in the air?"

She said, 'Then I'm fifteen minutes late."

😍

Some Golf Ironies

Golf balls are like eggs. They are white, are sold in a box of twelve, and you need to buy them every week.

Don't buy a putter until you've had a chance to throw it.

Never try to keep more than 300 separate thoughts in your mind during your swing.

When your shot has to carry over a water hazard, you can either hit one more club or two more balls.

If you're afraid a full shot might reach the green while the foursome ahead of you is still putting out, you have two options: you can immediately shank a lay-up or you can wait until the green is clear and top a ball halfway there…

The less skilled the player is, the more likely he is to share his ideas about the golf swing.

No matter how bad you are playing, it is always possible to play worse.

Everyone replaces his divot after a perfect approach shot.

A golf match is a test of your skill against your opponent's luck.

Nonchalant putts count the same as chalant putts.

It's not a gimme if you're still away.

The shortest distance between any two points on a golf course is a straight line that passes directly through the center of a very large tree.

You can hit a two-acre fairway 10% of the time and a two-inch branch 90% of the time.

If you really want to get better at golf, go back and take it up at a much earlier age.

Since bad shots come in groups of three, a fourth bad shot is actually the beginning of the next group of three.

When you look up, causing an awful shot, you will always look down again at exactly the moment when you ought to start watching the ball if you ever want to see it again.

Every time a golfer makes a birdie, he must subsequently make two triple bogeys to restore the fundamental equilibrium of the universe.

If you want to hit a 7 iron as far as Tiger Woods does, simply try to lay up just short of a water hazard.

A ball you can see in the rough from 50 yards away is not yours.

If there is a ball on the fringe and a ball in the bunker, your ball is in the bunker. If both balls are in the bunker, yours is in the footprint.

It's easier to get up at 6:00 AM to play golf than at 10:00 to mow the yard.

A good drive on the 18th hole has stopped many a golfer from giving up the game.

Golf is the perfect thing to do on Sunday because you always end up having to pray a lot.

A good golf partner is one who's always slightly worse than you are that's why I get so many calls to play with friends.

If there's a storm rolling in, you'll be having the game of your life.

To calculate the speed of a player's downswing, multiply the speed of his back-swing by his handicap; i.e., back-swing 20 mph, handicap 15, downswing = 300 mph.

There are two things you can learn by stopping your back-swing at the top and checking the position of your hands: how many hands you have, and which one is wearing the glove.

Hazards attract; fairways repel.

It's amazing how a golfer who never helps out around the house will replace his divots, repair his ball marks, and rake his sand traps.

If your opponent has trouble remembering whether he shot a six or a seven, he probably shot an eight (or worse).

It takes longer to learn to be a good golfer than it does to become a brain surgeon. On the other hand, you don't get to ride around on a cart, drink beer, or eat hot dogs if you are performing brain surgery.

😍

Tigers Woods Jokes

Top 10 Tiger Woods jokes on the Web

1. Apparently, the only person who can beat Tiger Woods with a golf club is his wife.
2. What's the difference between a car and a golf ball? Tiger can drive a ball 400 yards.
3. Tiger Woods was injured in a car accident as he pulled out of his driveway early Friday morning. It was Woods' shortest drive since an errant tee shot at the US Open.
4. What was Tiger Woods doing out at 2.30 in the morning? He'd gone clubbing.
5. Tiger Woods crashed into a fire hydrant and a tree. He couldn't decide between wood and iron.
6. Perhaps Tiger should be using a driver?
7. This is the first time Tiger's ever failed to drive 300 yards.
8. Apparently, Tiger admitted this crash was the closest shave he's ever had. So Gillette has dropped his contract.
9. Tiger Woods wasn't seriously injured in the crash. He's still below par though.
10. Tiger Woods is so rich that he owns lots of expensive cars. Now he has a hole-in-one.

😍

Golf To Stay Fit

An 80-year-old man goes to the doctor for a check-up. The doctor is amazed at what good shape the guy is in and asks, "How do you stay in such great physical condition?"

"I'm a golfer," says the old guy, "and that's why I'm in such good shape. I'm up well before daylight and out golfing up and down the fairways.

"Well," says the doctor, "I'm sure that helps, but there's got to be more to it. How old was your dad when he died?"

"Who said, my dad's dead?"

The doctor is amazed. "You mean you're 80 years old and your dad is still alive. How old is he?"'

"He's 103 years old," says the old golfer. "In fact, he golfed with me this morning, and that's why he's still alive ..... he's a golfer too!!"

"Well," the doctor says, "that's great, but I'm sure there's more to it than that. How about your dad's dad? How old was he when he died?"

"Who said my grandpa's dead?"

Stunned, the doctor asks, "You mean you're 80 years old and your grandfather is still living!? Incredible, how old is he?"

"He's 128 years old," says the old golfer.

The doctor is getting frustrated at this point, "So, I guess he went golfing with you this morning too?"

"No! Grandpa couldn't go this morning because he's getting married today."

At this point, the doctor is close to losing it, "Getting married! Why would a 128-year-old guy want to get married in the first place?"

"Who said he wanted to? The bride is pregnant, that is why!!!!!"

😍

Did you hear Phil Mickelson called Tiger's wife asking how to beat him?

😍

What do Phil Mickelson, Jaimee Grubbs, Kalaka Moquin and Rachel Uchitel all have in common?

They all played a round with Tiger Woods.

😍

What does Tiger Woods and a seal cub have in common? They both get clubbed by Norwegians.

😍

Take Up Golf !!!

My wife told me it was about time that I learned to play golf.

It's a game where you chase a little ball all over the country when you are too old to chase women.

So, I went to see Mr. Jones and asked him if he would teach me how to play.

He said, "Sure, you've got balls don't you?"

"Yes, but on cold mornings they are hard to find."

"Bring them to the clubhouse tomorrow and we will tee off."

"What's tee off?"

"It's a golf term and we have to tee off in front of the clubhouse."

"Not for me," I said. "You can tee off in front of the clubhouse, but I'll tee off behind the barn somewhere."

"No, no, a tee is a little thing about the size of your finger." "Yeah,

I've got one of those."

"Well, you stick it in the ground and put your ball on top of it."

"You play golf sitting down? I always thought you stood up and walked around."

"You do, you're standing up when you put your ball on the tee."

Well folks, I thought that was stretching things a bit too far and I said so.

He said, "You've got a bag haven't you?" "Sure."

"Your balls are in it, aren't they?" "Of course," I told him.

"Well, can't you open your bag and take one out?"

"I suppose I could, but I'll be damned if I am going to." "Don't you have a zipper on your bag?"

"No, I am the old-fashioned type."

"Do you know how to hold your club?"

Well, after 65 years, I should have some sort of an idea and I told him so.

He said, "You take your club in both hands..."

I knew right then he didn't know what he was talking about. Then he said, "Swing it over your shoulder..."

That's not me at all. That's my brother he's talking about. He asked, "How do you hold your club?"

Before I thought about it, I said, "With two fingers." He said that wasn't right.

He got behind me, put two arms around me, and said for me to bend over and he would show me.

Well, he couldn't catch me there. I didn't spend four years in the Navy for nothing.

He said, "You hit the ball with your club and it soars and soars..."

I could well imagine that.

". . and when you're on the green . . ." "What's the green?"

"That's where the hole is." "Sure you're not colour blind?"

"Then you take your putter in your hands..." "What's a putter?"

"That's the smallest club made." "That's what I got, a putter."

"And with it, you put your ball into the hole." I corrected him,

"You mean the putter."

"No, the ball. The hole isn't big enough for the ball and putter too."

Well, I've seen holes big enough for a horse and wagon.

"Then," he said, "after you finish with the first hole, you go on to the next 17."

Well, he certainly wasn't talking about me. After two holes I'm shot to hell.

"You mean you can't make 18 holes in one day?" "Hell no! It takes me 18 days to make one hole! "Besides, how do I know when I am in the 18th hole?" "The flag will go up!"

Well, golfing is not for me!

😍

Golf Ball

In My Hand, I Hold A Ball,
White And Dimpled, Rather Small. Oh, How Bland It Does Appear,
This Harmless Looking Little Sphere.

By Its Size, I Could Not Guess,
The Awesome Strength It Does Possess. But Since I Fell Beneath Its Spell,
I've Wandered Through The Fires Of Hell.

My Life Has Not Been Quite The Same, Since I Chose To Play This Stupid Game. It Rules My Mind For Hours On End,
A Fortune It Has Made Me Spend.

It Has Made Me Yell, Curse And Cry, I Hate Myself And Want To Die.
It Promises A Thing Called Par, If I Can Hit It Straight And Far.

To Master Such A Tiny Ball, Should Not Be Very Hard At All.
But My Desires The Ball Refuses, And Does Exactly As It Chooses.

It Hooks And Slices, Dribbles And Dies, And Even Disappears Before My Eyes. Often It Will Have A Whim,
To Hit A Tree Or Take A Swim.

With Miles Of Grass On Which To Land, It Finds A Tiny Patch Of Sand.
Then Has Me Offering Up My Soul, If Only It Would Find The Hole.

It's Made Me Whimper Like A Pup, And Swear That I Will Give It Up.
And Take To Drink To Ease My Sorrow,
But The Ball Knows ... I'll Be Back Tomorrow.

Stand proud you noble swingers of clubs and losers of balls......

😍

Bedroom golf... Here are the rules of the game.

1. Each player should furnish his own equipment for play - normally one club and two balls.
2. Play on the course should be approved by the owner of the hole.
3. Unlike outdoor golf, the object is to get the club in the hole and keep the balls out.
4. For the most effective play, the club should have a firm shaft. Course owners are permitted to check the shaft stiffness before play.
5. Course owners reserve the right to restrict club length to avoid damage to the hole.
6. The object of the game is to take as many strokes as necessary until the course owner is satisfied that the play is complete. Failure to do so may result in being denied permission to play the course again.
7. It is considered bad form to begin playing the hole immediately upon arrival at the course. The experienced player will normally take time to admire the entire course with special attention to the well-formed bunkers.
8. Players are cautioned not to mention other courses they have played, or are currently playing, to the owner of the course being played. Upset course owners have been known to damage players' equipment for this reason.
9. Players are encouraged to bring proper rain gear for their own protection.
10. Players should assure themselves that their match has been properly scheduled, particularly when a new course is being played for the first time. Previous players have been known to become irate if they discover someone else playing on what they considered to be a private course.

11. Players should not assume that a course is in shape for play at all times. Some players may be embarrassed if they find the course to be temporarily under repair. Players are advised to be extremely tactful in this situation. More advanced players will find alternative means of play when this is the case.
12. The course owner is responsible for manicuring and pruning any bush around the hole to allow for improved viewing of, alignment with, and approach to the hole.
13. Players are advised to obtain the course owner's permission before attempting to play the back nine.
14. Slow play is encouraged. However, players should be prepared to proceed at a quicker pace, at least temporarily at the course owner's request.
15. It is considered outstanding performance, time permitting, to play the same hole several times in one match.

😍

Many years ago in Scotland, a new game was invented. It was ruled 'Gentlemen Only...Ladies Forbidden' - and thus, the word GOLF entered into the English language.

😍

A guy was playing golf one day when he got lost. He saw a lady up ahead of him and went to her and said, "Can you please help me, I don't know what Hole I'm on?" She told him "You are one hole behind me. I'm on 7; you're on 6." He thanked her and continued playing golf. Later, he got lost again. He saw the same lady and went to her again kind of embarrassed. "I'm sorry to bother you again but I'm lost; can you please tell me what hole I'm on. "She told him, "You are one hole behind me. I'm on 14; you are on 13." Again, he thanked her and continued playing golf.

When he finished, he saw her in the clubhouse. He went up to her and asked if he could buy her a drink for helping him out. She accepted. As they were drinking and talking, he asked her what she did for a living. "I'm in sales," she said. He replied, "No kidding; so am I." "What do you sell?" She responded that it was too embarrassing to tell; but after he kept pleading to know what she sold, she finally said that she would tell him if he promised not to laugh. He promised.

She said, "I sell sanitary napkins. "He immediately fell to the floor laughing hysterically. She said, "You promised you wouldn't laugh." He replied (still with tears in his eyes), "I'm sorry, but I couldn't help it. I sell toilet paper. I'm still one hole behind you."

😍

Here is an actual sign posted at a golf club in Scotland.

Back Straight, Knees Bent, Feet Shoulder Width Apart. Form A Loose Grip.

Keep Your Head Down! Avoid A Quick Back Swing. Stay Out Of The Water.

Try Not To Hit Anyone.

If You Are Taking Too Long, Let Others Go Ahead Of You.

Don't Stand Directly In Front Of Others.

Quiet Please...While Others Are Preparing.

Don't Take Extra Strokes.

Well Done! Now, Flush The Urinal, Wash Your Hands And Go Outside,

And Tee Off.

😍

Why you don't play golf with your wife OR girlfriend?

A husband reluctantly agreed to play in the couples' alternate shot tournament at his club.

He teed off on the first hole, a par four, and blistered a drive 300 yards down the middle of the fairway.

Upon reaching the ball, the husband said to his wife:

"Just hit it toward the green, anywhere around there will be fine."

The wife proceeded to shank the ball deep into the woods.

Undaunted, the husband said "That's OK, Sweetheart" and spent the full five minutes looking for the ball.

He found it just in time, but in a horrible position.

He played the shot of his life to get the ball within two feet of the hole.

Still maintaining composure, the husband summoned all his skill and holed the shot from the bunker.

He took the ball out of the hole and, while walking off the green, put his arm around his wife and calmly said, "Honey, that was a bogey five, and that's OK, but I think we can do better on the next hole"

To which she replied, "Don't bitch at me, only 2 of those 5 shots were mine."

Man Killed on Golf Course

A foursome of guys is waiting at the mens' tee while a foursome of women is hitting from the ladies' tee.

The ladies are taking their time. When the final lady is ready to hit her ball, she hacks it 10 feet. Then she goes over and whiffs it completely.

Then she hacks it another ten feet and finally hacks it another five feet. She looks up at the patiently waiting men and says apologetically, "I guess all those 'f***ing' lessons I took over the winter didn't help."

One of the men immediately responds, "Well, there you have it! You should have taken golf lessons instead!".

He never even had a chance to duck.

😍

Hardest Putt

An older couple is playing in the annual club championship. They are playing in a playoff hole and it is down to a six-inch putt that the wife has to make. She takes her stance, and her husband can see her trembling.

She putts and misses, they lose the match. On the way home in the car her husband is fuming, "I can't believe you missed that putt! That putt was no longer than my 'willy'.

The wife just looked over at her husband and smiled and said, "Yes dear, but it was much harder!"

😍

Quite a Knock

A fellow tees off, and slices terribly. He sees the ball fly past a stand of trees and then hears a shriek.

He runs over and finds a woman knocked out cold. The man runs back to the clubhouse and shouts, "Is there a doctor here?"

"I'm a doctor," another man says, rising. "What's the trouble?"

"I just hit a woman with a golf ball out there and she's unconscious!"

"Well where did you hit her?" the doctor asks. "Between the first

and second holes."

"Oh my," the doctor says, shaking his head. "That doesn't leave much room for stitches!"

😍

Genie's Wish

A couple was golfing one day on an exclusive golf course lined with million-dollar houses. Off the third tee, the wife hit the ball right through the window of the biggest house on the course. Embarrassed, they ran up to the house and knocked on the door. A voice said, "Come on in."

Entering the house, they saw glass all over the floor, a broken bottle lying in the foyer, and a man sitting on the couch.

"Are you the people who broke my window?" he asked. "Yes we

are, but we're very sorry," the husband said.

"Actually I wanted to thank you." The man replied. "I'm a genie who was trapped for a thousand years inside that bottle you broke. Since you've released me, I'm allowed to grant two wishes

- one for you and one for myself."

"Wow!" the husband replied. "In that case, I want a million dollars a year for the rest of my life."

"Granted." The genie told him.

"Now for my wish...I've been trapped in that bottle, and without a woman, for a thousand years, so my wish is to sleep with your wife."

The husband looked at his wife, and then shrugged, "Well, we did get a lot of money, so I guess I don't care."

The genie took the wife upstairs and ravished her for hours. When they were finally done, he rolled over, looked at the wife, and asked, "How old is your husband?"

"Thirty-five," she replied. "And he still believes in genies? That's amazing!"

Loft

Three guys are golfing with the club pro. First guy tees off and hits a dribbler about 60 yards. He turns to the pro and says,

"What did I do wrong?" The pro says, "Loft."

The next guy tees off and hits a duck hook into the woods. He asks the pro, "What did I do wrong?"

The pro says, "Loft."

The third guy tees off and hits a slice into a pond. He asks the pro, "What did I do wrong?"

The pro says, "Loft."

As they`re walking to their balls, the first guy finally speaks up.

He says to the pro, "The three of us hit completely different tee shots, and when we asked you what we did wrong you gave the same exact answer each time. What is `loft?`"

The pro says, "L-O-F-T: Lack Of Fucking Talent."

😍

Wrong one??

An important senator arranges to use an escort service and winds up with a beautiful Japanese girl who speaks no English. They go into his hotel room and start having sex and she gets into it like there`s no tomorrow! She starts yelling the same Japanese word over and over and making faces and he can tell he`s driving her crazy! He`s never had it so good. The next morning, he`s golfing with the Japanese ambassador, and he makes a birdie. He suddenly remembers the word that the Japanese woman kept yelling out loud the night before, and he yells it out.

The ambassador looks at him strangely, looks at the pin, and says, "No, that was the right hole."

Tennis

Q: Why are zero scores in tennis called 'love'?
A: In France, where tennis first became popular, a big, round zero on the scoreboard looked like an egg and was called 'l'oeuf,' which is French for 'egg.' When tennis was introduced in the US, Americans pronounced it 'love.'

😍

Friendship Among Women & Men

A woman didn't come home one night. The next morning, she told her husband that she had slept over at a friend's house.

The man called his wife's 10 best friends. None of them knew anything about it.

FRIENDSHIP among Men

A man didn't come home one night. The next morning, he told his wife that he had slept over at a friend's house. The woman called her husband's 10 best friends. Eight confirmed that he had slept over, and two said he was still there.

😍

Humour & Games

Playing Bridge

A cleaning woman was applying for a new position. When asked why she left her last employment, she replied, "Yes, sir, they paid good wages, but it was the most ridiculously undignified place I ever worked.

They played a game called Bridge, and last night a lot of folks were there. As I was about to bring in the refreshments, I heard a man say, "Lay down and let's see what you've got." Another man said, "I've got strength but no length."

Another man says to the lady, "Take your hand off my trick!"

I pretty near dropped dead just then, when the lady answered, "You jumped me twice when you didn't have the strength for one raise."

Another lady was talking about protecting her honour and two other ladies were talking and one said, "Now it's time for me to play with your husband and you can play with mine."

Well, I just got my hat and coat and as I was leaving, I hope to die if one of them didn't say, "Well, I guess we'll go home now. This is the last rubber."

Cricket

A lady walked into a Police Station and the desk Sergeant said, "Can I help you?"

"Yes," she said, "I'd like to report a case of sexual assault." "Where did it happen?" the Sergeant asked.

"In the park just down the road," she replied. "Can you describe what happened?"

"Yes, I was walking along the footpath in the park near the trees when a man jumped out of the bushes and dragged me in there, removed my underwear then he dropped his pants to his knees and had his way with me." "Could you give me a description of him?" "Yes, he was wearing white shoes, long white trousers, a white shirt and he had these two big, long pads from his feet up to and over his knees, one on each leg."

“Sounds to me like he was a cricketer, most probably a batsman,” said the Sergeant. “Yes,” said the lady, “He was an English Cricketer.”

“That’s very observant,” said the Sergeant, “You worked that out from his accent?”

“No,” she replied. “I worked it out because he wasn’t in for very long.”

😍

Humour & Relationships

A Rushed Marriage

A man met a beautiful blonde lady and he decided he wanted to marry her right away.

She said, "But we don`t know anything about each other."

He said, "That`s all right, we`ll learn about each other as we go along."

So she consented and they were married, and went on a honeymoon to a very nice resort. One morning they were laying by the pool, when he got up off of his towel, climbed up to the 10 Meter board and did a two-and-a-half tuck gainer, this was followed by three rotations in the jackknife position, where he straightened out and cut the water like a knife. After a few more demonstrations, he came back and lay down on the towel.

She said, "That was incredible!"

He said, "I used to be an Olympic diving champion. You see, I told you we`d learn more about ourselves as we went along."

So she got up, jumped in the pool, and started doing laps. After about thirty laps she climbed back out and lay down on her towel hardly out of breath.

He said, "That was incredible! Were you an Olympic endurance swimmer?"

"No." she said, "I was a hooker in Venice and I worked both sides of the canal."

😍

A very elderly couple is having an elegant dinner to celebrate their 75th wedding anniversary. The old man leans forward and says softly to his wife "Dear, there is something that I must ask you. It has always bothered me that our tenth child never quite looked like the rest of our children. Now I want to assure you that these 75 years have been the most wonderful experience I could have ever hoped for, and your answer can not take that all that away. But... I must know, did he have a different father?"

The wife drops her head, unable to look her husband in the eye, she paused for a moment and then confessed. "Yes. Yes, he did." The old man is very shaken, the reality of what his wife was admitting hit him harder than he had expected. With a tear in his eye, he asks "Who?.. Who was he? Who was the father?"

Again the old woman drops her head, saying nothing at first as she tried to muster the courage to tell the truth to her husband. Then, finally, she says "You."

An Irish daughter had not been home for over 5 years.

Upon her return, her father cussed her. "Where have ye been all this time? Why did ye not write to us, not even a line? Why didn't ye call? Can ye not understand what ye put yer old mum thru?

The girl, crying, replied, "Sniff, sniff....dad. ...I became a prostitute "

"Ye what!!? Out of here, ye shameless harlot! Sinner! You're a disgrace to this family."

"OK, dad-- as ye wish. I just came back to give mum this luxurious fur coat, title deed to a ten-bedroom mansion plus a savings certificate for $5 million. For me little brother, this gold Rolex and for ye daddy, the sparkling new Mercedes limited edition convertible that's parked outside plus a membership in the country club ... (takes a breath) ..... and an invitation for ye all to spend New Year's Eve on board me new yacht in the Riviera, and "

"Now what was it ye said ye had become?" says dad.

Girl, crying again, "Sniff, sniff a prostitute dad! Sniff, sniff."

"Oh! Be Jesus! Ye scared me half to death, girl! I thought ye said a Protestant. Come here and give yer old man a hug!"

😍

Four insurance companies in Competition.

One comes up with a slogan,

"Coverage from cradle to coffin." second one tries to improve on that with, "Coverage from the womb to the tomb."

Not to be outdone, the third one comes up with, "From the sperm to the worm."

The fourth insurance company really thought hard and almost gave up the race, but finally came up with,

"From the erection to the resurrection. "

😍

Six Affairs

The 1st Affair

A married man was having an affair with his secretary. One day they went to her place and made love all afternoon. Exhausted, they fell asleep and woke up at 8 PM. The man hurriedly dressed and told his lover to take his shoes outside and rub them in the grass and dirt.

He put on his shoes and drove home. 'Where have you been?' his wife demanded. "I can't lie to you," he replied, "I'm having an affair with my secretary. We had sex all afternoon. &#39" She looked down at his shoes and said: "You lying bastard! You've been playing golf!'"

The 2nd Affair

A middle-aged couple had two beautiful daughters but always talked about having a son. They decided to try one last time for the son they always wanted. The wife got pregnant and delivered a healthy baby boy. The joyful father rushed to the nursery to see his new son. He was horrified at the ugliest child he had ever seen.

He told his wife: 'There no way I can be the father of this baby. Look at the two beautiful daughters I fathered! Have you been fooling around behind my back?" The wife smiled sweetly and replied: "No, not this time!'

The 3rd Affair

A mortician was working late one night. He examined the body of Mr. Schwartz, about to be cremated, and made a startling discovery. Schwartz had the largest private part he had ever seen!

“I'm sorry Mr. Schwartz,” the mortician commented, “I can't allow you to be cremated with such an impressive private part. It must be saved for posterity.

So, he removed it, stuffed it into his briefcase, and took it home. 'I have something to show you won't believe,' he said to his wife, opening his briefcase.

“My God!” the wife exclaimed, “Schwartz is dead!”

The 4th Affair

A woman was in bed with her lover when she heard her husband opening the front door. “Hurry,” she said, “stand in the corner.” She rubbed baby oil all over him, then dusted him with talcum powder.

“Don't move until I tell you,” she said. “Pretend you're a statue.

“What' s this?” the husband inquired as he entered the room.

“Oh it's a statue,” she replied. “The Smiths bought one and I liked it so I got one for us, too.” No more was said, not even when they went to bed.

Around 2 AM the husband got up, went to the kitchen and returned with a sandwich and a beer.

“Here,” he said to the statue, “Have this. I stood like that for two days at the Smiths and nobody offered me a damned thing.”

The 5th Affair

A man walked into a cafe, went to the bar and ordered a beer.

“Certainly, Sir, that'll be one cent.” “One Cent?” the man exclaimed. He glanced at the menu and asked: “How much for a nice juicy steak and a bottle of wine?”

“A nickel,” the barman replied. “A nickel?” exclaimed the man.

“Where is the guy who owns this place?” The bartender replied: ”Upstairs, with my wife.”

The man asked: “What' s he doing upstairs with your wife?” The bartender replied: 'The same thing I'm doing to his business down here.”

The 6th Affair

Jake was dying. His wife sat at the bedside. He looked up and said weakly: “I have something I must confess.” “There’s no need to,” his wife replied.

“No,” he insisted, “I want to die in peace. I slept with your sister, our best friend, her best friend, and your mother!” “I know,” she replied. “Now just rest and let the poison work.”

😍

Morris, an 82-year-old man, went to the doctor to get a medical examination. A few days later, the doctor saw Morris walking down the street with a gorgeous young woman on his arm.

A couple of days later, the doctor spoke to Morris and said,

“You're really doing great, aren't you?”

Morris replied, “Just doing what you said, Doc: ‘Get a hot mamma and be cheerful.”

The doctor said, “I didn't say that... I said, 'You've got a heart murmur; be careful.”

😍

Woman asks: If I sleep with three men, everyone calls me a slut. But when a man sleeps with ten women, everyone calls him a real man. How come . . .

Confucius replies: It's very simple. "When one lock can be opened by three different keys, it's a bad lock. But when one key can open ten different locks, we call it a MASTER KEY "

😍

Several years ago, I returned home from a trip just when a storm hit, with crashing thunder and severe lightning. As I came into my bedroom at about 2 a.m., I found my two children in bed with my wife, Karey, apparently scared by the loud storm. I resigned myself to sleep in the guest bedroom that night.

The next day, I talked to the children and explained that it was OK to sleep with Mom when the storm was bad, but when I was expected home, please don't sleep with Mom that night. They said OK.

After my next trip several weeks later, Karey and the children picked me up at the terminal at the appointed time. Since the plane was late, everyone had come into the terminal to wait for my plane's arrival, along with hundreds of other folks waiting for their arriving passengers.

As I entered the waiting area, my son saw me, and came running shouting, "Hi, Dad! I've got some good news!"

As I waved back, I said loudly, "What's the good news?"

Alex shouted, "Nobody slept with Mommy while you were away this time!"

The airport became very quiet, as everyone in the waiting area looked at Alex, then turned to me, and then searched the rest of the area to see if they could figure out exactly who his Mom was.

😍

That, My Friends, Is A Positive Attitude!

A very tall man walks into a bar, and a lady recognizes him as a real Rugby player. They start to talk and eventually go back to his place.

They start to kiss, and the man takes off his shirt. On his arm, he has a tattoo that says REEBOK.

"What's that for?" the lady questions. "Oh, I have this so that when I'm on TV, people will see my tattoo, and Reebok pays me." Then the man takes off his trousers, and on his leg, he has a tattoo that says NIKE.

What's that?' the lady questions again." Just like the Reebok tattoo, I get paid when this tattoo is seen on TV." Then the man drops his underwear and, on his penis, he has a tattoo that says AIDS.

The lady screams: "Don't tell me you have AIDS!" The man replies: "No, no...!!! Calm down...!!! It will read ADIDAS in a minute."

😍

A businessman in the first-class cabin asked the drop-dead-gorgeous flight attendant, "What's your name, Miss ?"

"Angela Benz, sir." Businessman: "Lovely name ... any relation to Mercedes Benz?"

"Yes sir, very close." Businessman: "How close?" "Same price."

😍

A Canadian salesman checked into a futuristic hotel in Tokyo, Japan. Realizing he needed a haircut before the next day's meeting, he called down to the desk clerk to ask if there was a barber on the premises.

“I'm afraid not, sir,” the clerk told him apologetically, “but down the hall from your room is a vending machine that should serve your purposes.”

Skeptical but intrigued, the salesman located the machine, inserted 15.00 Yen, and stuck his head into the opening, at which time the machine started to buzz and whirl.

Fifteen seconds later the salesman pulled out his head and surveyed his reflection, which reflected the best haircut of his life.

Two feet away was another machine with a sign that read, 'Manicures, 20.00 Yen'.

'Why not?' thought the salesman. He paid the money, inserted his hands into the slot, and the machine started to buzz and whirl. Fifteen seconds later he pulled out his hands and they were perfectly manicured.

The next machine had a sign that read, 'This Machine Provides a Service Men Need When Away from Their Wives, 1 Yen.'

The salesman looked both ways, put one Yen in the machine, unzipped his fly, and with some anticipation, stuck his manhood into the opening. When the machine started buzzing, the guy let out a shriek of agony and almost passed out. Fifteen seconds later it shut off.

With trembling hands, the salesman was able to withdraw his tender unit, which now had a button sewn neatly on the end.

😍

Voted Best Joke In Ireland (And Maybe In The World)!

John O'Reilly hoisted his beer and said, "Here's to spending the rest of me life, between the legs of me wife !" That won him the top prize at the pub for the best toast of the night! He went home and told his wife, Mary, "I won the prize for the best toast of the night." She said, "And what was your toast?"

John said, "Here's to spending the rest of my life, sitting in church beside me wife."

"Oh, that is very nice indeed, John !" Mary said. The next day, Mary ran into one of John's drinking pals on the street corner. The man chuckled leeringly and said, "John won the prize the other night at the pub with a toast about you, Mary."

She said, "Aye, he told me, and I was a bit surprised me-self. You know, he's only been in there twice in the last four years. Once I had to pull him by the ears to make him come, and the other time he fell asleep."

One Monday morning a mailman is walking the neighborhood on his usual route. As he approaches one of the homes he noticed some cars were in the driveway. His wonder was cut short by Bob, the homeowner, coming out the front door, stepping around empty beer and liquor, bottles.

"Wow, Bob, looks like you guys had one hell of a party last night!" the mailman says.

Bob, in obvious pain, replies, "Actually we had it Saturday night. This is the first I have felt like moving since 4 am Sunday morning.

We had about fifteen couples from around the neighborhood over for some weekend fun and it got a bit wild. Hell, we got so drunk around midnight that we started playing Who Am I?"

"Is that a game?" the mailman asks. "How do you play that?"

"Well, all the guys go in the bedroom and we come out one at a time with a sheet covering us and only our 'privates showing through a hole in the sheet. Then the women try to guess who it is."

The mailman laughs and says, "Damn, I'm sorry I missed that."

"Well, that's why I came out to talk to you," Bob says. "You better lay low for a few days, since your name came up seven times and several of the guys are now looking for you."

😍

A petrol station owner in Louisiana was trying to increase his sales. So, he put up a sign that read, "Free Sex with Fill-Up."

Soon John pulled in, filled his tank and asked for his free sex. The owner told him to pick a number from 1 to 10.

If he guessed correctly, he would get his free sex. John guessed 8, and the proprietor said, "You were close. The number was 7. Sorry. No sex this time." A week later, John, along with his friend, a Jew, pulled in for another fill-up. Again he asked for his free sex.

The proprietor again gave him the same story and asked him to guess the correct number. John guessed 2 this time. The proprietor said, "Sorry, it was 3. You were close, but no free sex this time." As they were driving away, the Jew said to the John, "I think that game is rigged, and he doesn't really give away free sex." John replied, "No it is genuine. It's not rigged at all. My wife won twice last week."

😍

Hunter was 4 years old and was staying with his grandfather for a few days. He'd been playing outside with the other kids, when he came into the house and asked, "Grandpa, what's that called when two people sleep in the same bedroom and one is on top of the other?"

His Grandpa was a little taken aback, but he decided to tell him the truth. "Well, Hunter, it's called sexual intercourse."

"Oh," Little Hunter said, "OK," and went back outside to play with the other kids. A few minutes later he came back in and said angrily, "Grandpa, it isn't called sexual intercourse. It's called Bunk Beds. And Jimmy's mom wants to talk to you."

😍

A woman was walking down the street when she was accosted by a particularly dirty and shabby-looking homeless woman who asked her for a couple of dollars for dinner.

The woman took out her wallet, extracted ten dollars and asked, "If I give you this money, will you buy some chocolate with it instead of dinner?"

"No, I had to stop sweets years ago", the homeless woman replied.

"Will you use it to go shopping instead of buying food?" the woman asked.

"No, I don't waste time shopping", the homeless woman said. "I need to spend all my time trying to stay alive."

"Will you spend this on a beauty salon instead of food?", the woman asked.

"Are you NUTS!" replied the homeless woman. "I haven’t had my hair done in 20 years!"

"Well," said the woman, "I'm not going to give you the money. Instead, I'm going to take you out for dinner with my husband and myself tonight.

The homeless woman was astounded. "Won't your husband be furious with you for doing that? I know I'm dirty and I probably smell pretty disgusting."

The woman replied, "That's okay. It's important for him to see what a woman looks like after she has given up shopping, salon and chocolates.

😍

After a tiring day, a commuter settled down In his seat and closed his eyes.

As the train rolled out of the station, the young woman sitting next to him pulled out her cell phone and started talking in a loud voice:

"Hi sweetheart. It's Sue. I'm on the train.

Yes, I know it's six thirty and not four thirty, but I had a long meeting.

No, honey, I'm not with Kevin from the accounting office or the boss".

"No sweetheart, you're the only one in my life. Yes, I'm sure, cross my heart!"

Fifteen minutes later, she was still talking loudly when the man sitting next to her had enough, he leaned over and said into the phone, "C'mon Sue, hang up the phone and come back to bed."

Sue doesn't use her cell phone in public anymore.

😍

A man was granted two wishes by God, He asked for the best drink & the best woman ever.

The next moment he got Mineral water & Mother Teresa.

😍

There are 3 kinds of men in this world.

- Some remain single and make wonders happen.
- Some have girlfriends and see wonders happen.
- Rest get married and wonder what happened!

😍

Wives are magicians. They can change anything into an argument.

😍

Why do women live a Better, Longer & Peaceful Lives, as compared to men?

A very INTELLIGENT student replied: "Because Women don't have a wife!"

😍

"Honey," said this husband to his wife, "I invited a friend home for supper."

"What? Are you crazy? The house is a mess, I haven't been shopping, all the dishes are dirty, and I don't feel like cooking a fancy meal!"

"I know all that," he said.

"Then why did you invite a friend for supper?" "Because the poor fool's thinking about getting married"

😍

Cool Message By A Wife

Dear Mother-in-law, don't teach me how to handle my children. I am living with one of yours and he needs a lot of improvement!

I Will Think About It: When a married man says, I'll think about it - what he really means is that he doesn't know his wife's opinion yet.

Talking In Sleep

A lady says to her doctor: "My husband has a habit of talking in his sleep. What should I give him to cure it?"

The doctor replies: "Give him an opportunity to speak when he's awake!"

😍

One day George's dad bought a robot. The robot was special in that it could detect a lie and would slap the person who lied on the face.

George returned late from school that day and his dad asked him," Son why are you late from school?"

George answered, "Dad we had extra classes today."

Much to his astonishment the Robot jumped up and slapped George on his face.

His dad told him "This robot is special in that he can detect a lie and will then slap the person who lied now come on tell me the truth, why are you late?"

"Dad I went for a movie", "Which movie?" "The Ten Commandments," S-p-la-tt George got a tight slap on the face from the robot.

"Sorry dad, I lied again, honestly I went for an adult movie ."

Dad: "Shame on you son when I was your age, I never used to do such shameful things." Splatt, the dad gets a tight slap on the face from the robot.

Hearing all this, George's mother comes walking out of the kitchen saying, "After all he is your son, he will be like you." To which the robot steps up and gives a resounding slap on George's mother's face.

😍

Voted the Best Joke for 2006

For his birthday, little Josh asked for a 10-speed bicycle.

His father said, "Son, we'd give you one, but the mortgage on this house is $280,000 & your mother just lost her job. There's no way we can afford it."

The next day the father saw little Joshua heading out the front door with a suitcase. So he asked, "Son, where are you going?"

Little Josh told him, "I was walking past your room last night & heard you telling Mom you were pulling out. Then I heard her tell you to wait because she was coming too.

And I'll be damned if I'm staying here by myself with a $280,000 mortgage & no bike!"

😍

Humour & Women

A girl wanting to be recruited during World War II was required to fill in an application form. In the space opposite' Previous Occupation, she entered 'Prostitute'. The Recruiting Sergeant informed her that she could not be enrolled with this sort of occupation and advised that she rephrase it.

After much thought, she wrote, 'Demolition of Temporary Erections'.

She was immediately recruited into the 'SAPPERS

😍

Recent Miss Universe Interview Miss World Questions –

AMERICA

Question: Ms. America, how do you describe a male organ in your country?

Ms. America: Well, I can say that male organs in America are like gentlemen.

Question: How can you say so?

Ms. America: Because it stands every time it sees a woman.

SPAIN

Question: Ms. Spain, how do you describe a male organ in your country?

Ms. Spain: Male organs in our country are like our very own Bullfight or Toro (Bull)

Question: How can you say so?

Ms. Spain: Because it charges every time it sees an opening.

PHILIPPINES

Question: Ms. Philippines, how do you describe a male organ in your country?

Ms .Philippines: Well, I can say that male organs in our country are like gossip or rumors.

Question: How can you say so?

Ms. Philippines: Because it passes from mouth to mouth......

SAUDI ARABIA

Question: Ms. Soudi Arabia, how do you describe a male organ in your country?

Ms. Saudi: Well, I can say that male organs in Saudi are like thieves.

Question: How can you say so?

Ms. Saudi: Because they like to enter through the back door.....

INDIA

Question: Ms. India, how do you describe a male organ in your country?
Ms. India: Well, I can say the male organs in India are like labourers.
Question: How can you say so?
Ms. India: Because it works day and night......

MALAYSIA

Question: Ms. Malaysia, how do you describe a male organ in your country?
Ms. Malaysia: Well, I can say that Male Organs in Malaysia are like Proton cars.
Question: How can you say so?
Ms. Malaysia: Look tough but actually very soft

SINGAPORE

Question: Ms. Singapore, how do you describe a male organ in your country?
Ms. Singapore: Well, I can say that the male organ in Singapore is very Kiasu (Afraid to lose).
Question: How can you say so?
Ms. Singapore: It always wants to rush in quick and leave 15 minutes before the show is over.

😍

Not Naughty At All.

The Importance of the BRA

Q: Bra which became the American President and inspired the whole world?
A: ABRAham Lincoln!

Q: Which bra is very important for any vehicle?
A: BRAke

Q: Which is the striped BRA?
A: zeBRA

Q: Poisonous BRA?
A: coBRA

Q: Mathematical BRA?
A: algeBRA

Q: Sunsign BRA?
A: liBRA

Q: Magical BRA?
A: aaBRA ka daBRA

Q: Religious BRA?
A: BRAhmin!

Q: Metallic bra?
A: BRAss

Q: Anjelina Jolie's Bra?
A: BRAd pit...

Q: Botany BRA?
A: BRAnch

Q: Marketing BRA?
A: BRAnd!

Q: Puctuation bra?
A:BRAcket

Q: Scary bra?
A:GhaBRAahat!! !!

Q: A room where BRA's are kept?
A: LiBRAry

Q: You forgot BRAndy! of all - things!!!

AND U THOUGHT ONLY WOMEN USE A BRA !!!

😍

Natural Blonde!

"Miss Jones, we can`t employ you as a model," the editor from the men`s magazine explained. "It`s too obvious that your blonde hair isn`t natural since the hair between your legs is black."

The model picked up a paperweight and slammed it down on the editor`s fingers.

"What the hell did you do that for!" he exploded.

She smiled sweetly and said, "Look at your fingers. They`re turning black, right? And they`ve only been banged once."

😍

The greatest Erection - Taj Mahal. So sad, Mumtaz Mahal didn't live to see Shah Jahan's greatest erection.

😍

Pregnant Jane

Since Jane is eight months into her pregnancy, John has to slccp on the floor to avoid any regrettable mistake, which might happen pretty easily, for he has been desperate for sex for quite a while now.

Just before lying down on the bed, she glances at him and sees poor John curled up on the floor, eyes staring widely into the empty air, filled with hopeless desire. Feeling sorry for her husband, Jane opens the top drawer of the cabinet, takes out a hundred rupee and gives it to him.

She says, "Awww, you're so depressed, here, take this and go to the woman next door, and she will let you sleep with her tonight. But remember that this happens only once. Don't think about it or ask me to do this again."

John rolls his eyes in disbelief, but afraid that she may change her mind, he grabs the money and leaves quickly.

A few minutes later, he returns, hands the money back to Jane and says with much disappointment, "She said this is not enough, she wants five hundred bucks."

Jane's face slowly turns red with anger, "Damn that bitch! When she was pregnant and her husband came over here I only charged him a hundred.

😍

Mother: Do u know the meaning of Mangalsutra? Daughter: Yes, it is the license to enjoy Kamasutra.

😍

A Woman has a man in it; Mrs. has Mr. in it; Female has male in it; She has he in it; Madam has Adam in it; No wonder men always want to be inside women!

John: What's the difference between Confidence and Confidential?

George: U are my son I'm Confident. Ur friend is also my son, that's Confidential.

Pregnant !!!

An extraordinarily handsome man decided he had the God-given responsibility to marry the perfect woman so they could produce children beyond comparison. With that as his mission, he began searching for the perfect woman. After a diligent, but fruitless, search up and down the east coast, he started to head west. Shortly thereafter he met a farmer who had three stunning, gorgeous daughters that positively took his breath away. So he explained his mission to the farmer, asking for permission to marry one of them.

The farmer simply replied, "They're all lookin' to get married, so you came to the right place. Look them over and select the one you want."

The man dated the first daughter. The next day the farmer asked for the man's opinion.

"Well," said the man, "She's just a weeeeee bit, not that you can hardly notice, but pigeon-toed."

The farmer nodded and suggested the man date one of the other girls; so the man went out with the second daughter. The next day, the farmer again asked how things went.

"Well," the man replied, "She's just a weeeee bit, not that you can hardly tell, cross-eyed."

The farmer nodded and suggested he date the third girl to see if things might be better. So he did.

The next morning the man rushed in exclaiming, "She's perfect, just perfect! She's the one I want to marry!" So they were wed right away.

Months later the baby was born. When the man visited the nursery he was horrified: the baby was the ugliest, most pathetic human you can imagine. He rushed to his father-in-law asking how such a thing could happen considering the parents."Well," explained the farmer, "She was just a weeeee bit, not that you could hardly tell, pregnant when you met her."

😍

All the Worries get initiated with "W"...

> Who?
> Why?
> What?
> When?
> Which?
> Whom?
> Where?
> War...
> Wine...
> Whisky...
> Women...
> Wealth...
> And finally ....
> agreeable or not......WIFE...

😍

Cinderella

Cinderella is now 95 years old. After a fulfilling life with the now-dead prince, she happily sits upon her rocking chair, watching the world go by from her front porch, with a cat named Bob for companionship.

One sunny afternoon out of nowhere appeared the fairy godmother. Cinderella said, "Fairy Godmother, what are you doing here after all these years"?

The fairy godmother replied, "Cinderella, you have lived an exemplary life since I last saw you. Is there anything for which your heart still yearns?"

Cinderella was taken aback, overjoyed, and after some thoughtful consideration, she uttered her first wish:

"The prince was wonderful, but not much of an investor. I'm living hand to mouth on my disability cheques, and I wish I were wealthy beyond comprehension. Instantly her rocking chair turned into solid gold."

Cinderella said, "Ooh, thank you, Fairy Godmother."

The fairy godmother replied, "It is the least that I can do. What do you want for your second wish?"

Cinderella looked down at her frail body, and said, "I wish I were young and full of the beauty and youth I once had."

At once, her wish became reality, and her beautiful young visage returned. Cinderella felt stirrings inside her that had been dormant for years.

And then the fairy godmother spoke once more: "You have one more wish; what shall it be?"

Cinderella looks over to the frightened cat in the corner and says, "I wish for you to transform Bob, my old cat, into a kind and handsome young man."

Magically, Bob suddenly underwent so fundamental a change in his biological make-up that, when he stood before her, he was a man so beautiful the likes of him neither she nor the world had ever seen.

The fairy godmother said, "Congratulations, Cinderella, enjoy your new life." With a blazing shock of bright blue electricity, the fairy godmother was gone as suddenly as she appeared.

For a few eerie moments, Bob and Cinderella looked into each other's eyes. Cinderella sat, breathless, gazing at the most beautiful, stunningly perfect man she had ever seen.

Then Bob walked over to Cinderella, who sat transfixed in her rocking chair, & held her close in his young muscular arms. He leaned in close, blowing her golden hair with his warm breath as he whispered.

"Bet you're sorry now that you cut my nuts off".

😍

Humour n Men

Principal: What is 3 x 3?

Boy.: 9

Principal: What is 6 x 6?

Boy.: 36

And so it went with every question the Principal thought a 4th grade should know. The Principal looks at Madam and tells her, I think Boy can go to the 4th grade.

Madam says to the Principal, 'I have some of my own questions'. 'Can I ask him?'

The Principal and Boy both agreed. Madam asks,

Q: What does a cow have four of that I have only two?

A: Boy, after a moment 'Legs.'

Q: What is in your pants that you have but I do not have?

A: Boy: Pockets.'

Q: What starts with a C and ends with a T, is hairy, oval, Delicious and contains thin whitish liquid?

A: Coconut.

Q: What goes in hard and pink then comes out soft and sticky? The Principal's eyes open really wide and before he could stop he answer, Boy was taking charge.

A: Bubblegum

Q: What does a man do standing up, a woman does sitting down and a dog does on three legs?

The Principal's eyes open really wide before he could stop the answer.

A: Shake hands.

Q: You stick your poles inside me. You tie me down to get me up. I get wet before you do.

A: Tent.

Q: A finger goes in me. You fiddle with me when you're bored. The best man always has me first. The Principal was looking restless, a bit tense.

A: Wedding Ring.

Q: I come in many sizes. When I'm not well, I drip. When you blow me, you feel good.

A: Nose

Q: I have a stiff shaft. My tip penetrates. I come with a quiver.

A: Arrow

Q: What word starts with a 'F' and ends in 'K' that means a lot of heat and excitement?

A: Fire Truck.

Q: What word starts with a 'F' and ends in 'K' & if u don't get it, you have to use your hand?

A: Fork.

Q: What is it that all men have one of its longer on some men than on others, the pope doesn't use his and a man gives it to his wife after they're married?

A: SURNAME.

Q: What part of the man has no bone but has muscles, has lots of veins, like pumping, & is responsible for making love?

A: HEART.

The Principal breathed a sigh of relief and said to the teacher, 'Send this Boy to Stanford or Harvard... I got the last ten questions wrong myself.

😍

After having failed his exam a student goes and confronts his lecturer about it.

Student: "Sir, do you really understand anything about the subject?"

Professor: "Surely I must. Otherwise, I would not be a professor!"

Student: "Great, well then I would like to ask you a question. If you Can give me the correct answer, I will accept my mark as is and go. If You however do not know the answer, I want you to give me an "A" for the Exam. "

Professor: "Okay, it's a deal. So what is the question?"

Student: "What is legal, but not logical; logical but not legal; and neither logical nor legal?"

Even after some long and hard consideration, the professor cannot give The student an answer, and therefore changes his exam mark into an "A", as agreed.

Afterward, the professor calls on his best student and asks him the Same question.

He immediately answers: "Sir, you are 63 years old and married to a 35-Year-old woman, which is legal, but not logical.

Your wife has a 25-Year-old lover, which is logical, but not legal.

The fact that you have given your wife's lover an "A", although he really should have failed, is neither legal, nor logical."

😍

Humour n Festival

Things You Can Only Say At Christmas

1. Tying the legs together keeps the inside moist.
2. Smother the butter all over the breasts.
3. If I don't undo my trousers, I'll burst!
4. I've never seen a better spread!
5. I fancy a little dark meat for a change.
6. Are you ready for seconds yet?
7. It's a little dry, do you still want to eat it?
8. Just wait your turn, you'll get some!
9. Don't play with your meat!
10. Stuff it up between the legs as far as it will go.
11. Do you think you'll be able to handle all these people at once?
12. I didn't expect everyone to come at the same time!
13. You still have a little bit on your chin.
14. How long will it take after you put it in?
15. You'll know it's ready when it pops up.
16. Just pull the end and wait for the bang.
17. That's the biggest bird I've ever had!
18. I'm so full, I've been gobbling nuts all morning.
19. Wow, I didn't think I could handle all that and still want more.
20. I prefer breasts to legs.

Humour & General

A woman and a man are involved in a car accident. It's a bad one. It's the woman's fault, but both of their cars are demolished but amazingly neither of them is hurt.

After they crawl out of their cars, the woman says; "So, you're a man. That's interesting. I'm a woman. Wow, just look at our cars! There's nothing left, but fortunately, we are unhurt. This must be a sign from God that we should meet and be friends and live together in peace for the rest of our days."

The man replied," I agree with you completely. This must be a sign from God!"

The woman continued, "And look at this, here's another miracle. My car is demolished, but this bottle of wine didn't break. Surely God wants us to drink this wine and celebrate our good fortune."

Then she hands the bottle to the man. The man nods his head in agreement, opens it, drinks half the bottle and then hands it back to the woman.

The woman takes the bottle, immediately puts the cap back on, and hands it back to the man.

The man asks, "Aren't you having any?"

She replies, "Nah. I think I'll just wait for the police to apprehend a drunk driver for rash driving."

Adam ate the apple, too! Men will never learn! - Always, women will conquer men forever and ever!!

Quiz Show

Jane was a first time contestant on the $65,000 quiz show. Lady luck had smiled in her favor, as Jane had a gained substantial lead over her opponents. She even managed to win the game but, unfortunately, time had run out before the show's host could ask her the big question.

Jane agreed to return the following day. Jane was nervous as her husband drove them home. "I've just gotta win tomorrow. I wish I knew what the answers are! You know I'm not going to sleep at all tonight. I will probably look like garbage tomorrow."

"Relax honey," her husband, Roger, reassured her, "It will all be OK."

Ten minutes after they arrived home, Roger grabbed the car keys and started heading out the door. "Where are you going?" Jane asked. "I have a little errand to run. I should be back soon."

After an agonizing 3-hour absence, Roger returned, sporting a very wide and wicked grin. "Honey, I managed to get tomorrow's question and answer!".

"What is it?" she cried excitedly.

"OK. The question is 'What are the three main parts of the male anatomy?' And the answer is 'The head, the heart, and the penis.' " The couple went to sleep with Jane, now feeling at ease, plummeting into a deep slumber.

At 3:30 a.m., however, Jane was shaken awake by Roger, who was asking her the quiz show question. "The head, the heart, and the penis," Jane replied groggily before returning to sleep. And Roger asked her again in the morning, this time as Jane was brushing her teeth. Once again, Jane replied correctly.

So it was that Jane was once again on the set of the quiz show. Even though she knew the question and answer, she could feel butterflies. The cameras began running and the host, after reminding the audience of the previous days' events, faced Jane and asked the big question.

"Jane, for $65,000, what are the main parts of the male anatomy? You have 10 seconds."

"Hmm, uhm, the head?" she said nervously.

"Very good. Six seconds." "Eh, uh, the heart?" "Very good! Four seconds." "I, uhh, ooooooohh, darn! My husband drilled it into me last night and I had it on the tip of my tongue this morning..."

"That's close enough!" said the game show host, “CONGRATULATIONS!!!"

😍

Polite Way To Pee

During one of her daily classes a teacher trying to teach good manners, asked her students the following question: 'Michael, if you were on a date having dinner with a nice young lady, how would you tell her that you have to go to the bathroom? Michael said, 'Just a minute I have to go pee.' The teacher responded by saying, 'That would be rude and impolite'. What about you Peter, how would you say it?' Peter said, 'I am sorry, but I really need to go to the bathroom. I'll be right back. 'That's better, but it's still not very nice to say the word bathroom at the dinner table.

And you, little Johnny, can you use your brain for once and show us your good manners?' 'I would say: Darling, may I please be excused for a moment? I have to shake hands with a very dear friend of mine, whom I hope you'll get to meet after dinner.' The teacher fainted!

😍

A man comes home, and finds his wife with his friend in bed. He shoots his friend and kills him.
Wife says :

"If you behave like this, you will lose ALL your friends".

😍

What is the definition of Mistress? Someone between the Mister and Mattress

😍

Husband asks: "Do u know that the meaning of WIFE is: Without Information Fighting Every-time
Wife replies: “No, It means”:
With Idiot For Ever

😍

What's the difference between stress, tension and panic? Stress is when a wife is pregnant,

Tension is when a girlfriend is pregnant. Panic is when both are pregnant.

😍

Grammar Teacher: Do you know the importance of a period?

Kid: Yeah, once my sister said she has missed one, my mom fainted, dad got a heart attack our driver ran away

😍

Jack was fixing a door and he found that he needed a new hinge, so he sent his wife, Mary, to BUNNINGS.

At BUNNINGS Mary saw a beautiful teapot on a top shelf while she was waiting for Charlie, from hardware, to finish waiting on a customer.

When Charlie was finished, Mary asked, "How much for the teapot?"

Charlie replied, "That's silver and it costs £300."

"My goodness that sure is a lot of money!" Mary exclaimed.

Then she proceeded to describe the hinge that John had sent her to buy, and Charlie went to the stockroom to find it. From the stockroom

Charlie yelled, "Mary, you wanna screw for that hinge?" Mary replied, "No, but I will for the teapot."

😍

Fire Man

A Jamaican fireman came home from work one day and said to his wife
"Ya know sumptin," womon, we have a wonderful new system at de Fire Station...

Bell 1 rings, we put on our jackets. Bell 2 rings, we slide down de pole.
Bell 3 rings, we jump on de engine and we's ready to go. So from

now on womon, when I say.......

"Bell one, I want you to strip naked. When I say Bell two, jump on de bed.
When I say Bell three, we's gonna mek love all tru de night girl.'"

The next night he came home and shouted:

"Bell One!," and his wife stripped naked. "Bell Two!," and she jumped on the bed. "Bell Three!," and they started to make love. After a few minutes, the wife yelled out "Bell Four!" "WOMON .... What DA hell is ' Bell Four'?" he asked.

She replied:

"ROLL OUT MORE HOSE, MON, YOU AIN'T NOWHERE NEAR DA FIRE!!!!"

😍

The Good Husband

Jack wakes up with a huge hangover after attending his company's Party. Jack is not normally a drinker, but the drinks didn't taste like alcohol at all. He didn't even remember how he got home from the party. As bad as he was feeling, he wondered if he did something wrong.

Jack had to force himself to open his eyes, and the first thing he sees is a couple of aspirins next to a glass of water on the side table. And, next to them, a single red rose!! Jack sits up and sees his clothing in front of him, all clean and pressed.

He looks around the room and sees that it is in perfect order, spotlessly clean. So is the rest of the house. He takes the aspirins, and cringes when he sees a huge black eye staring back at him in the bathroom mirror. Then he notices a note hanging on the corner of the mirror written in red with little hearts on it and a kiss mark from his wife in lipstick: "Honey, breakfast is on the stove, I left early to get groceries to make your favorite dinner tonight.

I love you, darling! Love, Jillian"

He stumbles to the kitchen and sure enough, there is hot breakfast, steaming hot coffee and the morning newspaper.

His 16-year-old son is also at the table, eating. Jack asks, "Son, what happened last night?"

"Well, you came home after 3 A.M., drunk and out of your mind You fell over the coffee table and broke it, and then you puked in the hallway, and got that black eye when you ran into the door. Confused, he asked his son, "So, why is everything in such perfect order and so clean? I have a rose, and breakfast is on the table waiting for me??"

His son replies, "Oh THAT... Mom dragged you to the bedroom, and when she tried to take your pants off, you screamed, "Leave me alone, I'm married!!"

😍

Before Marriage

Boy: Yes. At last. It was so hard to wait.
Girl: Do you want me to leave?

Boy: NO! Don't even think about it.
Girl: Do you love me?

Boy: Of course! Over and over!
Girl: Have you ever cheated on me?

Boy: NO! Why are you even asking?
Girl: Will you kiss me?

Boy: Every chance I get!
Girl: Will you hit me?

Boy: Are you crazy! I'm not that kind of person!
Girl: Can I trust you?

Boy: Yes.
Girl: Darling!

After Marriage

Simply read from bottom to top.

😍

Naughty mind... High expectations

It was Professor Smith's first day at St. Johns medical college as a faculty. Known for his teaching excellence, he made his entry into a classroom of 1st year medical students, where he received a warm welcome from the students, followed by their intro. To start with, he planned to put forth a question to the class.

He said, "Well students, before we start off with today's lecture, let me ask you a simple question on human anatomy". He gazed across the classroom, spotted a female student Suzie, and
said, "Tell me Suzie, which part of the human body grows 10 times its original size when excited?"

Hearing this question, Suzie's face grew pale in embarrassment, she replied:"You should be ashamed to ask such a question to a female. I am sorry, but I can't answer your, this question".

Thwarted by the girl's reply, Professor Smith rolled his sight around the classroom afresh, to find out if there was anyone else who could satisfy his query. This time he located a male student Henry, who had already raised his hand in affirmation to answer the question and allowed the lad to go ahead.

Henry answered: "Pupil of a human eye".

The Professor applauded for the boy's accurate answer; then turned back to Suzie and said: "Look, Suzie, I am sorry but, I must tell you three things.

(1) You lack knowledge

(2) You have a dirty mind and

(3) Your Expectations are too high !! **10** times...huh.

😍

A woman is at home when she hears someone knock at the door. She goes to the door and opens the door to see a man standing there. He asks the lady "Do you have a vagina".
She slams the door in disgust.

The next morning, she hears a knock at the door and it is the same man and he asks the same question of the woman "Do you have a vagina". She slams the door again.

Later that night when her husband gets home, she tells him what has happened for the last two days. The husband tells the wife in a loving and concerned voice "Honey I am taking tomorrow off to be home just in case this guy shows up again".

The next morning, they hear a knock at the door and both run for thc door. The husband says to the wife in a whispered voice "Honey, I'm going to hide behind the door and listen and if it is the same guy, I want you to answer yes to the question because I want to see where he is going with it". She nods yes to her husband and opens the door.

Sure, enough the same fellow is standing there and asks the same question. Do you have vagina?

"Yes," she says.

The man replies. "Good! Would You Mind Telling Your Husband To Leave My Wife's Alone And Start Using Yours?"

😍

Teacher: What do you want to become? Lil Johnny: Doctor !!
Teacher: Why?
Lil J: Coz it's the only profession where u can tell a woman to take off her clothes and ask her husband to pay for it.

😍

Woman complaining to Dentist: It's so painful, I'd rather have a baby than have a tooth removed.

Dentist: make up your mind soon! I'll adjust the chair accordingly.

😍

An old lady, 85, a virgin, is about to die. Wanted her tombstone to read: BORN A VIRGIN, LIVED A VIRGIN, DIED A VIRGIN.

The engraver shortened it to " RETURNED UNOPENED "

😍

A kid asked the priest "Father, what is your pastime? " The priest tapped the kid's shoulder and replied, "**Nun**, my child, **nun**."

😍

Something Funny For Friday!!!

A beautiful young woman, on an international flight, asked the priest beside her, "Father, may I ask a favour?"

"Of course, you may. What can I do for you?"

"Well, I bought this expensive electronic hair dryer that is well over the Customs limits and I'm afraid that they'll confiscate it from me. Is there any way that you could carry it through Customs for me?

Under your robes perhaps?"

"I would love to help you, dear, but I must warn you: I will not lie."

"With your honest face, Father, no one will question you."

When they got to Customs, the young lady let the priest go ahead of her.

The Customs Officer asked, "Father, do you have anything to declare?"

"From the top of my head down to my waist, I have nothing to declare."

The Officer thought this answer strange, so he asked, "And what do you have to declare from your waist to the floor?"

"I have a marvelous little instrument designed to be used on a woman, but which is, to date, unused."

Roaring with laughter, the Officer said, "God bless you, Father, go ahead."

😍

Mobile Number

A newly married husband saved his wife's mobile number on his mobile as "My life"

After one year of marriage, he changed the number to "My Wife"

After 2 years of marriage, he changed the number to "Home" After

5 years of marriage, he changed the number to "Hitler"

After 10 years of marriage, he changed the number to "Wrong Number"

😍

Arthritis

A drunken man who smelled of alcohol sat down on a subway next to a priest. The man's tie was stained, his face was plastered with red lipstick, and a half-empty bottle of gin was sticking out of his torn coat pocket. He opened his newspaper and began reading.

After a few minutes, the man turned to the priest and asked, “Say Father, what causes arthritis ?”

The priest replies, “My son, it's caused by loose living, being with cheap, wicked women, too much alcohol, contempt for your fellow man, sleeping around with prostitutes and a lack of a bath.”

The drunk muttered in response, “Well, I'll be damned,” then returned to his paper.

The priest, thinking about what he had said, nudged the man and apologized.

'I'm very sorry. I didn't mean to come on so strong. How long have you had arthritis ?'

The drunk answered, “I don't have it, Father. I was just reading here that the Pope does.”

MORAL: Make sure you understand the question before offering the answer.

😍

On Fridays, I Fish

After 35 years of marriage, a husband and wife came for counseling. When asked what the problem was, the wife went into a tirade listing every problem they had ever had in the years they had been married.

On and on and on neglect, lack of intimacy, emptiness, loneliness, feeling unloved and unlovable, an entire laundry list of unmet needs she had endured.

Finally, after allowing this for a sufficient length of time, the therapist got up, walked around the desk and after asking the wife to stand, he embraced and kissed her long and passionately as her husband watched - with a raised eyebrow.

The woman shut up and quietly sat down as though in a daze. The therapist turned to the husband and said, "This is what your wife needs at least 3 times a week. Can you do this ?"

"Well, I can drop her off here on Mondays and Wednesdays, but on Fridays, I fish."

😍

Jokes That Can Be Told In Church

Attending a wedding for the first time, a little girl whispered to her mother, 'Why is the bride dressed in white?" The mother replied, 'Because white is the color of happiness, and today is the happiest day of her life. 'The child thought about this for a moment then said, 'So why is the groom wearing black?

😍

At Sunday School they were teaching how God created everything, including human beings. Little Johnny seemed especially intent when they told him how Eve was created out of one of Adam's ribs. Later in the week, his mother noticed him lying down as though he were ill, and she said, ' Johnny, what is the matter?" Little Johnny responded, "I have pain in my side. I think I'm going to have a wife."

😍

40 yrs. of marriage

A married couple in their early 60s was celebrating their 40th wedding anniversary in a quiet, romantic little restaurant. Suddenly, a tiny yet beautiful fairy appeared on their table. She said, 'For being such an exemplary married couple and for being loving to each other for all this time, I will grant you each a wish. 'The wife answered, 'Oh, I want to travel around the world with my darling husband.' The fairy waved her magic wand and -poof!
- two tickets for the Queen Mary II appeared in her hands. The husband thought for a moment: 'Well, this is all very romantic, but an opportunity like this will never come again. I'm sorry my love, but my wish is to have a wife 30 years younger than me. 'The wife, and the fairy, were deeply disappointed, but a wish is a wish. So the fairy waved her magic wand and poof! The husband became 92 years old.

The moral of this story: Men who are ungrateful should remember that fairies are female.

😍

A woman came home, screeching her car into the driveway, and ran into the house. She slammed the door and shouted at the top of her lungs, “Honey, pack your bags. I won the lottery!”

The husband said, “Oh my God! What should I pack, beach stuff or mountain stuff?” “Doesn't matter,” she said. “Just get out.”

😍

Marriage is a relationship in which one person is always right, and the other is a husband.

😍

A wife was making a breakfast of fried eggs for her husband. Suddenly, her husband burst into the kitchen. "Careful," he said, "CAREFUL! Put in some more butter! Oh my gosh! You're cooking too many at once.

TOO MANY! Turn them! TURN THEM NOW! We need more butter. Oh my gosh! WHERE are we going to get MORE BUTTER? They're going to STICK! Careful. CAREFUL! I said be CAREFUL! You NEVER listen to me when you're cooking! Never! Turn them! Hurry up! Are you CRAZY? Have you LOST your mind? Don't forget to salt them. You know you always forget to salt them. Use the salt. USE THE SALT! THE SALT!"

The wife stared at him. "What in the world is wrong with you? You think I don't know how to fry a couple of eggs?" The husband calmly replied, "I just wanted to show you what it feels like when I'm driving."

😍

Some Very Smart and True Statements

Behind every successful man, there is a great woman and behind every great woman, there is a smart guy staring at her butt.

If you don't believe in oral sex, keep your mouth shut. Opinion is like an ass hole, everyone has one.

Chess players mate better.

Excuses are like asses: everyone has em and they all stink. Squirrel who runs up a woman's leg does not find nuts.

If I could rearrange the alphabet, I'd put you between F and CK.

Sex is the price women have to pay for marriage.

Marriage is the price men have to pay for sex. Impotence: Nature's way of saying "No hard feelings."

If you think sex is a pain in the ass, you're doing it wrong.

There are only two four-letter words that are offensive to men - **Don't** and **Stop**, unless they are used together.

The difference between a husband and a lover is the difference between day and night.

I love you in blue. I love you in red but most of all. I love you in bed.

Prostitution is a hole sale business.

A tight dress is like a barbed fence. It protects the premises without restricting the view.

What matters is not the length of the wand, but the magic in the stick.

Sex is like snow, you never know how many inches you are going to get or how long it is going to last.

I'm not attracted by a girl's mind ... But by what she doesn't mind.

Guns don't kill people... Husbands who come home early kill people.

Getting married is like getting into a bathtub. After you get used to it, it ain't so hot.

Marriage is the only war where you get to sleep with the enemy.

😍

This is one of the best comeback lines of all time.

It is a portion of National Public Radio (NPR) interview between a female broadcaster and US Marine Corps

General Reinwald who was about to sponsor a Boy Scout Troop visiting his military installation.

Female Interviewer: So, General Reinwald, what things are you going to teach these young boys when they visit your base?

General Reinwald: We're going to teach them climbing, canoeing, archery, and shooting.

Female Interviewer: Shooting! That's a bit irresponsible, isn't it?

General Reinwald: I don't see why, they'll be properly supervised on the rifle range.

Female Interviewer: Don't you admit that this is a terribly dangerous activity to be teaching children?

General Reinwald: I don't see how. We will be teaching them proper rifle discipline before they even touch a firearm.

😍

Female Interviewer: But you're equipping them to become violent killers.

General Reinwald: Well, Ma'am, you're equipped to be a prostitute, but you're not one, are you?

The radio went silent, and the interview ended.

😍